SUPERMAN ACTION COMICS
THE OZ EFFECT DELUXE EDITION

SUPERMAN ACTION COMICS
THE OZ EFFECT DELUXE EDITION

DAN JURGENS
ROB WILLIAMS
writers

VIKTOR BOGDANOVIC
DAN JURGENS * **RYAN SOOK** * **GUILLEM MARCH** * **WILL CONRAD**
JONATHAN GLAPION * **JAY LEISTEN** * **TREVOR SCOTT** * **SCOTT HANNA**
artists

MIKE SPICER
HI-FI
colorists

ROB LEIGH
letterer

NICK BRADSHAW and **BRAD ANDERSON**
collection cover artists

MIKE COTTON PAUL KAMINSKI Editors - Original Series ✷ ANDREA SHEA Assistant Editor - Original Series
JEB WOODARD Group Editor - Collected Editions ✷ ROBIN WILDMAN Editor - Collected Edition
STEVE COOK Design Director - Books ✷ DAMIAN RYLAND Publication Design

BOB HARRAS Senior VP - Editor-in-Chief, DC Comics
PAT McCALLUM Executive Editor, DC Comics

DIANE NELSON President ✷ DAN DiDIO Publisher ✷ JIM LEE Publisher ✷ GEOFF JOHNS President & Chief Creative Officer
AMIT DESAI Executive VP - Business & Marketing Strategy, Direct to Consumer & Global Franchise Management ✷ SAM ADES Senior VP & General Manager, Digital Services
BOBBIE CHASE VP & Executive Editor, Young Reader & Talent Development ✷ MARK CHIARELLO Senior VP - Art, Design & Collected Editions
JOHN CUNNINGHAM Senior VP - Sales & Trade Marketing ✷ ANNE DePIES Senior VP - Business Strategy, Finance & Administration
DON FALLETTI VP - Manufacturing Operations ✷ LAWRENCE GANEM VP - Editorial Administration & Talent Relations
ALISON GILL Senior VP - Manufacturing & Operations ✷ HANK KANALZ Senior VP - Editorial Strategy & Administration ✷ JAY KOGAN VP - Legal Affairs
JACK MAHAN VP - Business Affairs ✷ NICK J. NAPOLITANO VP - Manufacturing Administration ✷ EDDIE SCANNELL VP - Consumer Marketing
COURTNEY SIMMONS Senior VP - Publicity & Communications ✷ JIM (SKI) SOKOLOWSKI VP - Comic Book Specialty Sales & Trade Marketing
NANCY SPEARS VP - Mass, Book, Digital Sales & Trade Marketing ✷ MICHELE R. WELLS VP - Content Strategy

SUPERMAN: ACTION COMICS: THE OZ EFFECT–DELUXE EDITION

PEFC Certified
Printed on paper from
sustainably managed
forests and controlled
sources
PEFC/01-31-106   www.pefc.org

Only Human
PART 1

IT IS *SO* EASY TO RESENT HIM.

HUMAN BEINGS ARE COMPLEX AND CONFUSED, THEY ARE A CHURNING MASS OF DESIRES AND FEARS AT ANY GIVEN MOMENT. A WHITE NOISE OF BEMUSEMENT.

WE ARE NOT BINARY. GOOD AND EVIL WOULD BE BLISSFUL DEFINITIONS. UNATTAINABLE CERTAINTY. FOREVER OUT OF REACH.

HE, HOWEVER, IS GOOD.

IT IS *SO* EASY TO RESENT HIM...

ROB WILLIAMS *Writer*
GUILLEM MARCH *Artist*
HI-FI *Color*
ROB LEIGH *Letters*
GUILLEM MARCH *Cover*
NEIL EDWARDS AND JEROMY COX *Variant Cover*
PAUL KAMINSKI *Associate Editor*
MIKE COTTON *Editor*
EDDIE BERGANZA *Group Editor*

SUPERMAN created by Jerry Siegel and Joe Shuster. SUPERBOY created by Jerry Siegel. By special arrangement with the Jerry Siegel family.

CLARK...

CAN YOU HEAR ME?

I CAN HEAR YOU, LOIS. THE EARPIECE WORKS GREAT.

WHAT'S WRONG?

YOU'RE NOT HERE! THAT'S WHAT'S WRONG!

YOUR SON SAYS HELLO.

SAY HEY TO DAD FOR ME!

HEY, JON! I DID THE PACKING. I JUST... NEEDED TO GET OUT FOR A WHILE.

I'M WORRIED ABOUT YOU. YOU'VE BEEN THROUGH A LOT LATELY. GODSLAYER, THE REVENGE SQUAD, MXYZPT--

PLEASE DON'T SAY THAT NAME.

AND NOW THE MOVE TO METROPOLIS. LEAVING HAMILTON COUNTY. YOU NEED A BREAK.

WE NEED A BREAK. OUR LITTLE TRIP WASN'T ENOUGH.

NO... YOU'RE RIGHT, WE *HAVE* BEEN THROUGH A LOT LATELY...

AH!

⟨RUN! RUN! THEY'RE KILLING US!⟩*

*TRANSLATED FROM GEORGIAN. --Cotton

⟨WOLVES...⟩

⟨EVEN THE *ANIMALS* HAVE JOINED THEM!⟩

⟨AHHH!⟩

SIT!

HE PROBABLY THINKS THE MIND-TICK'S CONTROL IS DISTANCE RELATED.

IT'S NOT.

LET'S BE READY FOR THEM WHEN THEY RETURN.

PRIME ALL WEAPONS.

THINK, LEX.

YOU'RE THE SMARTEST MAN ON THE PLANET. YOUR CIRCUITRY'S *IN* THAT MIND-TICK. YOU MUST BE ABLE TO COME UP WITH A WAY TO BREAK THIS.

THE MIND-TICK CAN'T HAVE BEEN BUILT TO DEAL WITH APOKOLIPTIAN PHYSIOLOGY. AND THE MORE YOU USE THE APOKOLIPTIAN TECHNOLOGY...

YOUR WORDS...

YOU *CAN* FIGHT THIS.

GOT YOU.

I DON'T KNOW WHAT YOU'RE TALKING ABOUT! I WAS JUST TAKING ORDERS! HIS ORDERS!

IT'S NOT ME, I SWEAR!

HE HAS X-RAY VISION, YOU FOOL.

HE CAN PICK UP ALL SORTS OF ELECTROMAGNETIC FIELDS WITH THAT. INCLUDING THE ENERGY SIGNATURES OF YOUR MIND-TICKS.

I'VE PIERCED YOUR DISGUISES BEFORE, MACHINIST. I KNOW WHAT YOU'RE HIDING UNDERNEATH.

...

SO YOU KNOW MY TRUE FACES...

*SEE SUPERMAN: THE MEN OF TOMORROW. --P & C

SORRY.

GUESS I SEE THROUGH PEOPLE.

YOU ARE *NOT* HIM.

YOU WILL *NEVER* BE SUPERMAN.

EVEN WHEN YOU TRY TO DO GOOD, YOU CANNOT ESCAPE THE BASE INIQUITY OF YOUR RACE.

THIS IS JUST WHO YOU ARE. NO MATTER HOW HARD YOU TRY. CRAWLING AMIDST THE DETRITUS.

ALL OF YOU.

YOU ARE ONLY HUMAN. YOU WILL ONLY EVER *BE* HUMAN.

AND SOON YOU WILL BE GONE.

AH...

AH...

WITH HOPE FOR AN EVEN BETTER TOMORROW.

I HOPE YOU DON'T MIND JON COMING IN WITH ME FOR A BIT, PERRY.

ABLE TO ENJOY LIFE.

WE'RE HAVING THE APARTMENT PAINTED AND THE FUMES ARE OVERWHELMING.

MIND?

WHY WOULD I MIND GETTING A CHANCE TO START SHAPING MY GODSON INTO A REPORTER?

WHOA, CHIEF.

"I'M THINKING LI'L CLARKY WOULD RATHER BE A PRO QUARTERBACK LIKE ME, RIGHT?"

I'LL BET YOUR OLD MAN HAS TOLD YOU PLENTY ABOUT WHAT AN HONOR IT IS TO WORK WITH A STAR.

Uh-uh.

WHAT'S YOUR NAME AGAIN?

LOMBARD.

STEVE **LOMBARD**!

C'MON, KID. YOU **MUSTA** HEARD OF ME!

Um...

CHECK MY OFFICE AND YOU'LL SEE MY ROOKIE CARD AND SODER COLA GAME-OF-THE-WEEK MVP AWARD ON DISPLAY!

MAYBE ANOTHER TIME, MR. LOMBARD.

I'M SORTA WAITIN' FOR MY **DAD**.

TELL YOU WHAT, NEXT TIME YOU AND THE OLD MAN ARE FREE, I'LL GET US FIFTY-YARD-LINE SEATS TO A METEORS GAME.

THANKS FOR THE OFFER, STEVE.

I'LL CHECK THE CALENDAR AND GET BACK TO YOU.

CLARK, I CAN'T BEGIN TO TELL YOU HOW HAPPY I AM TO HAVE YOU KIDS LIVING BACK IN THE CITY AGAIN.

LIFE ISN'T THE SAME WITHOUT LOIS LANE AND CLARK KENT WORKING AT THE **PLANET**.

WAIT-- I GOT AN EVEN **BETTER** IDEA.

I'LL GET YOU AN OLD-SCHOOL, TOTALLY AUTHENTIC METEORS STEVE LOMBARD THROWBACK JERSEY!

MOST **AWESOME** THING A KID LIKE YOU COULD HOPE TO WEAR--GUARANTEED!

WHATTAYA SAY?

Uh...

IF HE ONLY KNEW...

...THAT JON HAS SOMETHING FAR BETTER TO WEAR?

AND ALREADY LEADS A LIFE...

WE'RE OFF FOR SOME LUNCH.

IT'S BIBBO'S SUPER BURGER DAY AT THE ACE O' CLUBS!

AWESOME!

WHOA. HEY, CHIEF, MY PHONE IS BLOWIN' UP.

MINE, TOO, OLSEN.

I'VE NEVER SEEN SO MANY SIMULTANEOUS ALERTS COME THROUGH.

OIL TANKER RUPTURED ON SHORE... PRISON RIOT IN THE MIDWEST...WORKPLACE SHOOTINGS...

ALASKAN COAST

4 BREAKING NEWS

WAR BREAKING OUT IN LOGAMBA...

RACIAL DISPUTES, TERRORIST ACTS, WIDESPREAD VIOLENCE EVERYWHERE...

THIS IS MORE THAN ANYONE CAN HANDLE! EVEN...

SUPERMAN!

MY NATURAL PARENTS DIED WITH KRYPTON.

YOU CAN'T *POSSIBLY* BE JOR-EL.

I *AM* YOUR *FATHER.*

FULL-SPECTRUM ANALYSIS, *KELEX.*

THE *WORKS.*

IDENTIFY THIS FRAUD.

UNDERSTAND YOUR DOUBT, KAL.

DESPITE YOUR SKEPTICISM, I ASK THAT YOU LISTEN TO MY STORY, FOR I SPEAK THE *TRUTH*.

KRYPTON *DIED*.

BUT I *SURVIVED*.

...ELEX WILL DO WHAT YOU SAY, BUT NOT UNTIL *I* ASK.

AFTER ALL, HE IS PROGRAMMED TO RESPOND TO HIS INVENTOR FIRST...

SIR.

...AND HIS INVENTOR'S PROGENY *SECOND*.

FULFILL HIS REQUEST, KELEX.

YES, SIR.

DNA SENSORS, RETINA SCAN AND VOICE ANALYSIS ARE *CONCLUSIVE*.

THE OZ EFFECT
PART TWO

DAN JURGENS WRITER **RYAN SOOK** ART

MAY I PRESENT *YOUR FATHER.*

JOR-EL OF *KRYPTON.*

HI-FI COLOR **ROB LEIGH** LETTERS

ROBSON ROCHA, DANIEL HENRIQUES & JASON WRIGHT COVER

NEIL EDWARDS & JEROMY COX VARIANT COVER

ANDREA SHEA ASSISTANT EDITOR

MIKE COTTON & PAUL KAMINSKI EDITORS

EDDIE BERGANZA GROUP EDITOR

SUPERMAN created by JERRY SIEGEL and JOE SHUSTER. BY SPECIAL ARRANGEMENT WITH THE JERRY SIEGEL FAMILY.

NO.

IT'S A *TRICK*.

LIKE WHEN MXYZPTLK PASSED HIMSELF OFF AS CLARK KENT.*

*SUPERMAN REBORN.
--Paul & Cotton

THEN HOW DID I KNOW WHERE TO FIND YOU WHEN WE FIRST MET?

OR KNOW TO BRING YOU HERE?

YOUR BOY IS GROWING UP FAST. YOU AND LOIS MUST BE PROUD.

THE MOTEL...*

FRIEND OR ENEMY IS TOO SIMPLE A TERM WHEN YOU CONSIDER THE LONG GAME.

*DC UNIVERSE: REBIRTH. --P & C

I HAVE BEEN WATCHING YOU ALL YOUR LIFE. MY GRANDSON AS WELL.

I STILL DON'T--!

HOW DID YOU--?

AMONG THEIR MANY FUNCTIONS, THESE CRYSTALS SERVE TO ARCHIVE OUR HOUSE'S *HISTORY*.

YOUR EXPERIENCES AND MEMORIES...

...AS WELL AS *MINE*.

LET US LOOK INTO THE PAST, WHEN I FOUGHT FOR KRYPTON'S FUTURE WITH THE SAME FERVOR AND DEDICATION YOU APPLY TO EARTH'S.

WE'RE GOING BACK...

TO A HAPPIER TIME.

OUR CONSCIOUSNESS WILL BE INSERTED INTO OUR ARCHIVED HISTORY.

WEEKS BEFORE KRYPTON'S DEMISE, WHEN I THOUGHT WE COULD BE SAVED.

THAT IS LOR-VAN, MY SCIENTIFIC BENEFACTOR AND YOUR MATERNAL GRANDFATHER.

KRYPTON IS DOOMED. PROJECT STARDRIVE WILL SAVE OUR CULTURE AND PEOPLE.

BUT... THE RESEARCH I FUNDED WAS SUPPOSED TO SAVE THE PLANET, JOR-EL.

NOT EVACUATE IT!

SAVING KRYPTON IS IMPOSSIBLE. I REALIZE THAT SPACE TRAVEL IS FORBIDDEN, BUT--

DEEMED ILLEGAL BECAUSE OF JAX-UR'S CRIMES!

AS THE PLANET'S LAST ASTRONAUT, I KNOW FULL WELL THAT THIS RESEARCH IS FORBIDDEN.

SAVING LIVES IS NEVER WRONG!

I'M PROVIDING HOPE!

THAT'S--!

YOUR BEAUTIFUL MOTHER, LARA, DAYS BEFORE YOUR BIRTH.

PLEASE, AT THIS TIME, ABOVE ALL OTHERS...

...I WANT THE TWO MOST IMPORTANT MEN IN MY LIFE TO GET ALONG.

DON'T YOU REALIZE THAT THE SCIENCE COUNCIL ALREADY CONSIDERS YOUR HUSBAND AN ALARMIST FOOL?

THOUGH I QUESTION HIS THEORIES, I POURED MILLIONS INTO HIS RESEARCH IN SUPPORT OF YOU, LARA.

BUT NOT FOR SPACE ARKS!

IF ZOD OR THE COUNCIL LEARNS OF THIS, YOU'LL BE ARRESTED!

I WILL NOT HAVE MY GRANDSON GROW UP WITH HIS FATHER EXILED TO THE PHANTOM ZONE!

KELEX!

I FUNDED YOUR DEVELOPMENT, SO YOU WILL RESPOND TO MY COMMANDS.

ERASE ALL OF THIS!

DESTROY EVERY BIT OF DATA ON PROJECT STARDRIVE!

DONE.

FATHER--?!

MY OWN GRANDFATHER DID THAT?

THE FIRST TIME I WAS BETRAYED.

IT WOULD NOT BE THE LAST.

YOU'LL THANK ME ONE DAY.

WHEN YOU'VE DOOMED ALL OF US?

NEVER!

THIS REALLY HAPPENED?

IT WAS NEVER AS SIMPLE AS THE SCIENCE COUNCIL REJECTING MY RESEARCH.

COUNTLESS WRONGS CONTRIBUTED TO OUR DESTRUCTION.

THEY ERASED MY DATA, BUT NOT MY MEMORY.

I REPROGRAMMED KELEX TO FOLLOW *MY* COMMANDS AND REBUILT WHAT I COULD.

NO ARMADA. JUST ONE SMALL SHIP.

HE WILL CARRY THE HISTORY, THOUGHTS AND DREAMS OF KRYPTON WITH HIM.

OUR LAST SHARED EXPERIENCE, KAL.

BUT, AS KRYPTON DIED, WE TOOK SOLACE IN KNOWING...

"...THAT YOU WERE TRAVELING TO A WORLD THAT WOULD WELCOME YOU WITH OPEN ARMS.

"ALL WE HOPED FOR WAS A QUICK, PAINLESS END.

"BUT *THAT* WAS NOT TO BE.

"ON THE VERGE OF DEATH...

"...IN THE SMALLEST INCREMENT OF TIME POSSIBLE, SOMETHING INTERVENED.

"IN A MOMENT FAR MORE HORRIFYING AND PAINFUL THAN ANYTHING I COULD IMAGINE...

"...I WATCHED YOUR MOTHER *DIE*.

"WHILE I LIVED."

THIS GOES AGAINST *EVERYTHING* I'VE EVER KNOWN.

THE CRYSTALS ON YOUR SHIP RECEIVED DATA UP TO THE MOMENT OF YOUR DEPARTURE.

THEY RECORDED KRYPTON'S DEMISE, NEVER KNOWING THAT FOR ME...

"...TIME STOPPED, EVEN AS EVERYONE AND EVERYTHING AROUND ME *DIED*.

"EVEN AS I EXPERIENCED THE UNIMAGINABLE...

"...I WAS *TAKEN*."

WHO COULD POSSIBLY--?

SOMETHING *BEYOND* US.

A BEING ABLE TO BEND REALITY TO HIS EVERY WHIM, THOUGH I DIDN'T WANT IT.

I WANTED TO BE WITH *LARA.*

DEATH WOULD HAVE BEEN FAR BETTER THAN WHAT CAME NEXT.

I WAS SAVED FOR A *REASON.*

WHY?

I THINK... I WAS SAVED TO BEAR WITNESS TO THE *TRUTH.*

WHAT TRUTH?

EARTH'S.

THE NATURE OF ITS *PEOPLE* AND WHAT THEY REALLY ARE.

IF YOU'RE REALLY WHO YOU CLAIM--

YOU STILL DON'T BELIEVE ME?

I WANT TO.

BUT...

...I'VE BEEN DECEIVED BEFORE.

THIS ALL SEEMS SO IMPOSSIBLE-- WITH SO MANY UNANSWERED QUESTIONS.

SUCH AS HOW *DID* I, LIKE YOU, *END* UP ON EARTH?

YOU ARRIVED TO FIND SAFETY IN THE LOVING EMBRACE OF THE KENTS.

THE LIGHT THAT SAVED ME CARRIED ME TO A VERY DIFFERENT PLACE.

THE MOST LAWLESS, DANGEROUS CITY EARTH HAD TO OFFER.

⟨IS HE ALIVE?⟩

⟨I THINK HE'S AN AMERICAN?⟩

⟨LOOK FOR MONEY!⟩

⟨NO.⟩

<We WILL HELP THE POOR MAN.>

<HELP HIM? WE SHOULD TURN HIM OVER TO KASSAM.>

<SO THAT BUTCHER CAN TORTURE HIM, HOLD HIM FOR RANSOM...>

<...OR SIMPLY KILL HIM?>

<NO.>

<IT IS RIGHTEOUS TO HELP THE WAYFARER.>

<WON'T KASSAM PUNISH US IF WE SAY NOTHING, MOTHER?>

<THESE STRANGE, GREEN SPLINTERS. I DARE REMOVE NO MORE.>

<THE STRANGER DOES NOT NEED A GUN IN HIS FACE, AAZIM.>

<HE NEEDS HELP.>

THE CITY MIGHT HAVE BEEN WAR-TORN, BUT THEY CARED FOR YOU.

SO THEY DID. NOT THAT I WANTED IT, KAL.

AT THE TIME, I WAS A DAMAGED, EMOTIONALLY EMPTY MAN.

"BUT SOMETHING WANTED ME ALIVE TO SEE HUMANITY FOR WHAT IT REALLY IS."

<I REGRET I CANNOT OFFER MORE, BUT FOOD IS SCARCE.>

LEAVE ME ALONE!

"I DIDN'T CARE IF I LIVED.

"AT LEAST NOT UNTIL A YOUNG BOY..."

<BUT I AM HUNGRY.>

<OUR HONORED GUEST WILL EAT FIRST, AAZIM.>

"HE MADE ME THINK OF YOU, KAL."

"I DIDN'T KNOW YOUR FATE. WERE YOU IN A HELLHOLE LIKE ME?"

"OR *WORSE?*"

〈GO. YOU MUST HIDE DURING THE DAY.〉

"I COULDN'T GO OUT TO FEEL THE SUN ON MY FACE.

"I SPENT DAYS IN THE DARK, THINKING ABOUT WHAT COULD HAVE BEEN.

"I WAS *ALONE.*"

"UNTIL..."

KASSAM'S ARMY NEEDS FOOD!   NOW!

"IN THE MIDST OF A CIVIL WAR, FOOD HAD BECOME A WEAPON.

"STARVATION, A TACTIC."

〈DID YOU SEE THEIR *GUNS?* THAT'S WHAT MAKES THEM *POWERFUL!*〉

〈THEY LEFT *NOTHING!* IT'S ALL WE *HAD!*〉

"I CONTINUED TO HEAL IN THE MIDST OF SCREAMS, GUNFIRE AND BODIES ROTTING IN THE STREETS.

"DEATH WAS *EVERYWHERE.*

"I COULDN'T STOP WORRYING ABOUT *YOU.*"

"ALL I WANTED WAS TO FEED A HUNGRY FAMILY.

"THE IDEA THAT SOMEONE COULD BE SO EVIL AS TO DENY A HUMAN BEING *FOOD*...

BRAKKT

...WAS COMPLETELY FOREIGN TO ME.

I COULD NOT FATHOM THE CONSEQUENCES TO COME.

⟨STEAL FROM *ME*...⟩

⟨...AND YOU *PAY*.⟩

CRACK

⟨DON'T HURT THE *BOY!*⟩

⟨HURT HIM?⟩

"AS THE SUN ROSE, I WAS TOO PREOCCUPIED TO REALIZE THAT THE KICK DIDN'T HURT."

THAK

⟨I WILL *REWARD* HIM!⟩

⟨YOU CAN BE *ONE* OF US, YOUNG ONE.⟩

⟨BE ONE WHO RULES THIS FORSAKEN PLACE.⟩

⟨TO EARN THAT EXALTED POSITION, YOU MUST *PUNISH* THE TRAITORS.⟩

⟨ALL OF THEM.⟩

⟨BUT...⟩

⟨DON'T *DO* THIS, AAZ!⟩

⟨*DON'T!*⟩

⟨YOU *KNOW* THEY VIOLATED MY LAW.⟩

⟨*PROVE* YOU DESERVE TO *JOIN* US.⟩

⟨I *CAN'T!*⟩

⟨...YOU *CAN.*⟩

⟨YES...⟩

RATT

MY GOD.

THERE WAS NO GOD PRESENT THAT DAY.

ONLY MAN'S CAPACITY FOR EVIL.

HA HAHH!

‹YOUR TURN.›

‹HOW...›

‹...COULD YOU *DO* THIS?›

"TO THIS DAY, I DON'T KNOW IF IT WAS AS SIMPLE AS BEING IN THE SUN...

"...OR IF MY CONTROLLER *LET* MY POWERS EMERGE.

"IN MY RAGE, I COULD NOT HOLD BACK."

‹WHY, AAZIM?›

WHY?!

"THAT'S WHEN I KNEW HUMANITY WAS **HOPELESS**.

"THAT THERE IS NO SAVING THEM FROM THEMSELVES.

BRATTA BRAT

"WITH THAT REALIZATION, I WAS TAKEN AGAIN."

THAT WAS **AWFUL**, I ADMIT.

BUT THAT HARDLY REPRESENTS ALL OF HUMANITY.

I WARNED KRYPTON.

THEY DID NOT LISTEN.

JUST AS EARTHERS WILL **NEVER** LISTEN TO YOU.

YOU CAN'T USE ONE TERRIBLE EVENT AS--

I EXPERIENCED **FAR** MORE THAN JUST ONE EVENT.

WHATEVER BROUGHT ME HERE MADE SURE OF THAT.

"IT SHOWED ME **EVERYTHING**."

THEY CLAIM BENEVOLENCE AS THEY ADVOCATE SEEMINGLY OBVIOUS IDEALS, BUT IN REALITY ARE UNENLIGHTENED *SAVAGES.*

CONQUEST, MATERIAL GAIN, SUBJUGATION AND SELF-INTEREST WILL FOREVER LIMIT THEM.

TRAITS SUCH AS THESE *DOOMED* KRYPTON.

BUT THESE PEOPLE OF *YOURS...*

...ARE *WORSE.*

THEY *DESERVE* WHAT'S COMING.

HAD I KNOWN THEY'D FOREVER IGNORE THE INSPIRATION *YOU* PROVIDE...

...I WOULD NOT HAVE SENT YOU HERE.

THEIR PEOPLE ARE SO MIRED IN THE ETERNAL DESPAIR OF THEIR OWN CREATION...

...THAT I AM SOMEWHAT AMAZED--AND PROUD--THAT YOU GREW TO BECOME THE MAN YOU ARE TODAY.

YOU'RE *WRONG.* I ALWAYS HAVE HOPE THAT--

OF *COURSE* YOU DO. JUST AS I HAD HOPE FOR KRYPTON.

LOOK WHERE IT GOT ME.

WHY *NOW?* WHAT ARE YOU TRYING TO SAY?

I MADE A GRAVE *MISTAKE* IN SENDING YOU HERE, SON.

FOR WHICH I AM *SORRY.*

...NUCLEAR POWER PLANT SABOTAGED...

...CHILD BEATEN TO DEATH FOR LUNCH MONEY...

SO MANY THINGS HAPPENING AT ONCE. LIKE THE WORLD IS COMING *UNGLUED.*

COINCIDENCE... OR IS SOMETHING *BIGGER* GOING ON?

BREAKING NEWS *TRAGIC DEATH*

LEVEL SEVEN *SCORE.*

...AFTERNOON OF *TERROR* IN A HOSPITAL AS...

WHERE'S *SUPERMAN* IN ALL OF THIS, CHIEF?

JIMMY, IF I KNOW HIM, I'LL BET HE'S RALLYING THE LEAGUE TO--

PLEASE DON'T--!

POK POK POK

GUNSHOTS?!

TAKE JON AND HEAD FOR THE BACK STAIRS, LOIS!

JON! GET OVER HERE BEFORE--

OH MY GOD!

BRAMM

THAT'S RIGHT. WE'RE *ALL GOIN'* TO SEE GOD.

TOGETHER.

"EARTH WILL DESTROY ITSELF, KAL."

DAN JURGENS STORY & BREAKDOWN ART   VIKTOR BOGDANOVIC PENCILS

--GOD.

PART II

BOGDANOVIC & TREVOR SCOTT INKS   NEIL EDWARDS & JEROMY COX VARIANT C
MIKE SPICER COLOR ROB LEIGH LETTERS   ANDREA SHEA ASST. EDITOR PAUL KAMINSKI & MIKE COTTON EDI
NICK BRADSHAW & BRAD ANDERSON COVER   EDDIE BERGANZA GROUP ED

PLEASE. RATHER THAN RESORT TO VIOLENCE, TELL ME WHAT YOUR PROBLEMS WITH THE *DAILY PLANET* ARE...

...AND WE'LL *FIX* THEM. TOGETHER.

HAVE TO BUY TIME.

HOPE THAT CLARK FIGURES OUT WHAT'S HAPPENING.

AND GETS HERE BEFORE IT'S TOO LATE.

YOU CAN'T TAKE BACK YOUR *LIES!*

THE WORLD MUST KNOW THAT YOU PRINT *FAKE NEWS* IN ORDER TO *CONTROL* US!

BULL!

IF THERE'S *ANYTHING* THIS PAPER AND I STAND FOR--IT'S THE *TRUTH!*

THAT'S A *LIE* AND YOU *KNOW* IT!

LET ME TELL YOUR SIDE OF THE STORY. I WANT TO *HELP* YOU.

I KNOW THE TRUTH. OZ SHOWED US WHAT'S REAL.

THAT YOU'RE HIDING THE TRUTH OF HOW *BAD* THINGS ARE.

OZ?

CLARK TOLD ME OZ COULD BE A THREAT, BUT WE HAD NO IDEA HE HAD *FOLLOWERS.*

OZ *UNDERSTANDS.*

KNOWS THAT FOR MOST--THERE IS *NO* TOMORROW.

BUDDY, THE ONLY THING I KNOW...

...IS YOU.

WHOOOOOOM BRAMM

THAT TAKES CARE OF THE LAUNCHERS.

NOW FOR THE MISSILES.

WE CAN'T *LEAVE*, UNCLE PERRY!

MOM *NEEDS* US!

YOUR MOM IS THE SMARTEST, MOST CAPABLE PERSON I KNOW, JON.

SHE'LL BE *FINE*.

BELIEVE IT.

DAILY PLAN

SKASSSH

SUPERMAN!

THIS HAPPENS RIGHT--

--GUH!--

BRAK

BWHMM

SKASH

HELLO, LOIS.

YOU'RE NOT SUPERMAN...

...WHO...

OH.

DID YOU SEE *THAT?!*

THAT MEANS LOIS IS OKAY, RIGHT?

SEE, JON? YOUR MOM IS JUST FI--! --JON?

MOM WOULDN'T WANT ME TO DUCK OUT ON UNCLE PERRY LIKE THAT...

...BUT SHE'D LIKE IT EVEN LESS IF HE SAW ME DOIN' *THIS.*

AND NOW THAT DAD IS HERE AND THE BUILDING IS EMPTY...

...THE COAST IS CLEAR FOR **SUPERBOY** TO HELP!

ONLY TWO LEFT.

CAN'T JUST KNOCK THEM OUT OF THE SKY.

CHEMICAL WEAPONS NEED SPECIAL CARE.

THE RESERVOIR TANK.

KRIPP

HAVE TO MAKE SURE THE GAS CAN'T ESCAPE.

TSSS

SO THAT NO ONE ELSE USES IT.

EVER.

BAD ENOUGH THE GOVERNMENT USES SUCH A HEINOUS TACTIC.

BUT THE REBELS ARE USING INNOCENT CIVILIANS AS SHIELDS.

MAKES ME WONDER IF JOR-EL--IF THAT'S WHO HE REALLY IS--

--IS RIGHT.

"...ARE YOU TELLING ME YOU DON'T *KNOW* WHERE MY SON IS?"

JONATHAN.

I RECOGNIZE THAT VOICE!

YOU'RE THE GUY THAT WAS COACHING ME IN THE FORTRESS!

YES. THE REASON I WAS ABLE TO ACCESS YOUR FATHER'S FORTRESS AND DO SO...

...IS BECAUSE I AM YOUR *GRAND-FATHER.*

FROM KRYPTON.

WH-WHAT? *HOW?*

DAD SAID HIS PARENTS DIED WHEN KRYPTON BLEW UP.

THAT WAS HIS UNDERSTANDING.

YOUR FATHER WARNS YOU TO BE WARY OF STRANGERS, BUT I HAVE SOMETHING THAT WILL PROVE MY IDENTITY.

LIKE WHAT?

A KRYPTONIAN CRYSTAL. ONE THAT CAN REVEAL YOUR PAST...

...AND *FUTURE.*

FOR *REAL?* THAT'S... *ME?*

IN A FEW YEARS, AT YOUR NEW HOME.

"WE HAVE A LOT TO DISCUSS, JON, BUT NOT HERE."

"WILL YOU COME TO THE FORTRESS WITH ME?"

COMPUTER, EMERGENCY OVERRIDE.

CLICK

OVERRIDE ACCEPTED. WELCOME, MISS JANET.

"DAD LETS YOU GO TO THE FORTRESS?"

A SHAME ABOUT J.B.

BUT THE CHAOS BRINGS US CLOSER TO THE END.

"OF COURSE, JON. WHEN YOU GET DOWN TO THE ESSENCE OF IT ALL..."

"...I BUILT THE PLACE."

METROPOLIS WILL DIE...

...SO OZ'S CHOSEN MIGHT LIVE.

HOW DID WE GET HERE? WE WERE JUST--

I HAVE METHODS THAT ALLOW ME TO TRAVEL INSTANTLY, JON. MECHANISMS I CREATED.

DO YOU SEE THAT STATUE? THAT WAS YOUR GRANDMOTHER AND ME BEFORE KRYPTON WAS DESTROYED.

BUT YOUR... I MEAN...IT'S GOT TWO...

EYES? YES, I KNOW. I WAS INJURED IN THE BLAST THAT DESTROYED MY WORLD.

I MUST ASK, JON. DO YOU LIKE YOUR HOME?

WELL, HAMILTON COUNTY WAS BETTER THAN METROPOLIS.

I AM REFERRING TO EARTH ITSELF, JON. AS LONG AS YOU LIVE HERE...

...YOU'LL HAVE TO HIDE YOUR TRUE NATURE BY WEARING THOSE GLASSES AND THAT SILLY CAP.

OZ EFFECT

PART FOUR

DAN JURGENS STORY & BREAKDOWN ART
VIKTOR BOGDANOVIC PENCILS
BOGDANOVIC, TREVOR SCOTT
& SCOTT HANNA INKS
MIKE SPICER COLOR · ROB LEIGH LETTERS
NICK BRADSHAW & BRAD ANDERSON COVER
NEIL EDWARDS & JEROMY COX VARIANT COVER
ANDREA SHEA ASSISTANT EDITOR
PAUL KAMINSKI & MIKE COTTON EDITORS

SUPERMAN created by JERRY SIEGEL and JOE SHUSTER.
SUPERBOY created by JERRY SIEGEL.
BY SPECIAL ARRANGEMENT WITH THE JERRY SIEGEL FAMILY.

GREEN ARROW AND BLACK CANARY TOOK DOWN A NEO-NAZI ARMS STASH.

SO I'M ON MY OWN.

KARA STOPPED A MASSIVE AMOUNT OF CROPS FROM BEING POISONED.

KONG KENAN DID THE SAME IN CHINA.

WHAT COULD POSSIBLY COMPEL SOMEONE TO POISON FOOD?

--CONFIRMED IT WAS NERVE GAS FIRED INTO THE CAPITAL, YOUR EXCELLENCY.

MAY I REMIND YOU THAT WE HAVE A FULLY FUNCTIONAL, LIMITED-AREA NUCLEAR DEVICE WE CAN EMPLOY AGAINST THE REBELS?

IF NOT FOR THE CAPED AMERICAN, BODIES WOULD LITTER THE STREETS.

WE MUST DO SO WHILE THE REBELS ARE STILL FAR FROM THE CITY.

VERY WELL. I WILL NOTIFY...

WAIT. IS THAT--?

WIND?

GYAHH!

NO MORE WASTING TIME.

NOT WHILE PEOPLE ARE DYING.

THESE MEN HAVE TO SETTLE THEIR DIFFERENCES...

...BEFORE IT'S TOO LATE.

WHA--?

YOUR *CONFLICT* ENDS TODAY.

TALK TO EACH OTHER.

NEGOTIATE.

THE KILLING.

STOPS.

NOW.

THEY WALLOW IN WEALTH WHILE OUR CHILDREN STARVE!

THESE PEOPLE ARE CRUDE AND INFERIOR.

TOO STUPID TO WORK IN OUR INDUSTRIES!

THEN YOU WILL *USE* YOUR WEALTH TO *EDUCATE* THEM.

HA!

AND *YOU* WILL TELL YOUR PEOPLE THAT THEY CAN'T JUST TAKE WHAT THEY WANT.

THEY MUST BE WILLING TO MAKE THE BEST OF THEIR LIVES AND LEARN.

IMPOSSIBLE.

YOU CLAIM TO CARE ABOUT YOUR *OWN* CHILDREN.

I NEED YOU TO CARE ABOUT *EACH OTHER'S.*

JON! WHERE ARE YOU, BUD?

IF HE'S ANYTHING LIKE HIS MOTHER, CURIOSITY GOT THE BETTER OF HIM AND HE'S FOLLOWING THE ACTION AROUND HERE.

INSTEAD OF GETTING TO SEE MY OLD JERSEY?

THAT'S HARD TO BELIEVE.

IT'S CRAZY OUT THERE, JIMMY. *DANGEROUS.*

I REALIZE THAT, CHIEF. THAT'S WHY...

"...I GAVE LOIS THE MEANS TO CALL IN THE CAVALRY."

NO LUCK REACHING CLARK AT THE FORTRESS. HE MUST BE KNEE-DEEP IN THE GLOBAL CHAOS.

I NEED SUPERMAN.

BUT OUR SON IS MISSING, AND I NEED TO USE ALL THE TOOLS AT MY DISPOSAL.

ZEEZEE

THE FORTRESS OF SOLITUDE. MOMENTS AGO.

WOW! THIS CITY IS BEAUTIFUL!

THIS IS NOT WHAT I ENVISIONED...

OR AGREED TO.

EVERY GUN, GRENADE, MACHETE... EVERY WEAPON WE HAD!

FROM *BOTH* SIDES? IT'S *LUNACY*!

IF YOU FIGHT NOW, YOU'LL DO SO WITH ROCKS AND STICKS.

ANOTHER REASON TO FIND *PEACE.*

DON'T--!

BWHOOM

NOW *SOLVE* THIS.

ZEEZEEE

JIMMY.

HE KNOWS NOT TO USE HIS SIGNAL WATCH UNLESS THERE'S BIG TROUBLE.

HAVE TO ASSUME THE WORST.

SO I SEE HOW *BAD* PEOPLE CAN BE?

THE *GAS!*

THE EVIL *MUST* BE WIPED AWAY!

WHATEVER EVIL YOU THINK YOU'RE ATTACKING...

...*YOU'RE* JUST AS BAD.

NOTHING WILL PASS THROUGH THOSE PIPES.

NOTHING.

YOU'RE RUINING *EVERYTHING!*

DON'T YOU UNDERSTAND?!

OZ WON'T SAVE YOU.

HE'S TRYING TO MAKE A POINT...

...AND USING *YOU* TO DO IT.

THE WORLD'S TURMOIL-- COORDINATED.

AND IT'S OZ PULLING THE STRINGS.

ZEEZEEE

JIMMY'S ALARM.

ZEEZEEE

I PRAY I'M NOT TOO LATE!

YOU CALLED HIM... **GRANDDAD?**

INDEED, HE DID.

MY GRANDSON IS AN INTELLIGENT YOUNG MAN.

YOU HAVE **NO RIGHT** TO TALK TO--

BUT IT'S **TRUE,** DAD!

HE'S **JOR-EL!**

CLARK.

IF THERE'S ANY CHANCE IT'S TRUE, YOU CAN'T ATTACK YOUR FATHER.

IT'S MORE THAN THAT, LOIS...

FOR **MONTHS** NOW WE'VE BEEN WARNED THAT SOMEONE WAS OUT THERE... SOMEONE DANGEROUS...

...AND IT'S TRUE. I'VE SEEN THE **PROOF.**

MR. OZ IS RESPONSIBLE FOR THE WORLD'S CHAOS...

...AND THIS MAN IS **OZ!**

WHY... WOULD HE **DO** THAT?

DAD, GIVE HIM A **CHANCE...**

...BECAUSE THIS IS ABOUT *YOU.*

WHERE--?

AT FIRST, IT WAS MY PRISON.

NOW MY HOME. FREE FROM THE RESTRAINTS OF TIME AND SPACE.

WHEN EARTH DIES...

...LIKE SO MANY DOOMED WORLDS BEFORE IT...

...THIS PLACE WILL PROVIDE SAFE HAVEN.

IF A THREAT OF THAT MAGNITUDE LOOMS OVER EARTH, I WON'T BE *HERE.*

I'LL BE *THERE.*

FIGHTING TO SAVE IT.

DO SO, AND YOU WILL DIE.

AS WILL YOUR WIFE AND CHILD.

I'VE HAD *ENOUGH* OF YOUR REFUSAL TO ACCEPT THE *TRUTH.*

AND IF YOU WON'T ACT TO SAVE YOURSELF AND YOUR FAMILY...

...*I WILL.*

SHRAK

I DON'T LIKE DOING THIS, BUT I *KNOW* WHAT'S COMING, KAL.

IT'S SO MUCH *BIGGER*--SO MUCH MORE *POWERFUL* THAN YOU.

I CAN *SAVE* YOU...

...IF YOU *LET* ME.

BUT WHO'S GOING TO SAVE ME FROM *YOU?*

KRYPTONITE...

...THE SINGLE MOST LETHAL WEAPON IN EXISTENCE...

...IS *YOURS* TO COMMAND...

...YET YOU USE IT AGAINST YOUR OWN *FLESH* AND *BLOOD?*

THE FORTRESS.

IF THE *BEING* THAT'S OUT THERE CAN SEND ME BACK HERE SO EASILY...

...HE'S AS POWERFUL AND DANGEROUS AS JOR-EL SAYS.

HE TOOK MY FATHER FROM THE BRINK OF DEATH.

BROKE HIM.

TWISTED HIM.

SOMEHOW MADE IT SEEM *RIGHT*...

...TO SHOW ME MAN AT HIS *WORST*.

BUT WHAT IF HE'S RIGHT?

ARE WE AS LOST AS HE SAYS?

WE SHOULD GET INSIDE, JON. WHO KNOWS WHEN THEY'LL BE BACK?

MOM, *LOOK!*

...SITUATION DESCRIBED AS *BEYOND HOPE.*

CLARK?

ARE YOU OKAY?

PEOPLE ARE LOSING HOPE, LOIS.

WHERE ARE YOU GOING, DAD?

BACK TO WORK.

...THEN WHAT DOES THAT MAKE *ME*?

SYSTEM CHECK COMPLETE. I AM UNCOMPROMISED.

HI-FI **ROB LEIGH** **FRANCIS MANAPUL** **JERRY ORDWAY & HI-FI**
color   letters   cover   variant cover

ANDREA SHEA **PAUL KAMINSKI** **EDDIE BERGANZA**
assistant editor   editor   group editor

BRUCE?

I DIDN'T HEAR THE BATPLANE APPROACHING.

NO...

...YOU DIDN'T.

LOOKS LIKE YOU WERE BUSY.

YOU CAN'T DO THIS, CLARK. YOU LOSING YOUR TEMPER, GETTING *RECKLESS*. IT'S NOT THE SAME FOR THE REST OF US. IT'S...

DANGEROUS? IS THAT WHY YOU'RE HERE, BRUCE? TO MAKE SURE THE *POWERFUL* ALIEN IS IN CHECK?

ARE YOU WORRIED ABOUT WHAT I'M CAPABLE OF?

NO.

HAS ANYBODY SEEN KENT?

GREAT CAESER'S GHOST! THE BOY'S BIG ENOUGH TO PLAY TIGHT END FOR THE METROPOLIS METEORS! HE CAN'T HAVE JUST VANISHED!

PRINT IS DEAD, THEY KEEP TELLING ME! TOUGH TO KEEP PRINT ALIVE IF AN EDITOR CAN'T FIND HIS DAMN REPORTERS FOR DAYS ON END!

I'D SAY IT'S AN 8.2, LOIS. IF YOU KNOW WHERE CLARK IS, I'D GET WORD TO...

I GOT THIS, JIMMY.

CLARK'S ON A STORY, PERRY. DEEP COVER.

WHAT? HE'S BEEN GONE FOR DAYS. WHY DIDN'T HE TELL ME?

NO TIME. HE HAD TO GO RIGHT AWAY OR LOSE THE SOURCE.

YEAH? WHAT'S THE STORY? HE WAS WORKING ON THE DOCKSIDE DEVELOPMENT.

CORRUPTION CLAIMS AGAINST SENATOR MCVAY.

I THOUGHT THAT WAS *YOUR* STORY?

WE'RE MARRIED, PERRY. WE'VE BEEN WORKING IT TOGETHER. THIS IS A BIG LEAD.

COVERING FOR YOUR HUSBAND, LOIS?

SOMETIMES YOU HAVE TO FOLLOW YOUR INSTINCTS. YOU KNOW THAT. EVEN IF THEY SEEM EXTREME.

SO, I GUESS THIS COMES DOWN TO ONE POINT, PERRY...

...DO YOU *TRUST* YOUR REPORTERS, OR *DON'T* YOU?

TELL KENT TO CALL ME THE MOMENT YOU HEAR FROM HIM.

I WOULDN'T WANT TO *COMPROMISE* HIM.

DAMMIT, CLARK. WHERE *ARE* YOU?

COOL

"SOMETIMES YOU HAVE TO FOLLOW YOUR INSTINCTS. EVEN IF THEY SEEM EXTREME."

THAT'S SOME GOOD ADVICE, MISS LANE.

SUPERMAN.

IT'S GOOD TO SEE YOU.

I JUST WISH IT WAS UNDER HAPPIER CIRCUMSTANCES.

SO DO I, HAL.

THANK YOU FOR THIS. I APPRECIATE IT.

YOU'RE ALWAYS WELCOME HERE. YOU KNOW THAT.

YOU'RE BACK.

I DIDN'T WANT TO WAKE JON.

DID YOU FIND IT? WHAT YOU WERE LOOKING FOR.

NO.

SOMETHING'S VERY WRONG, LOIS.

AND THIS ISN'T JUST ABOUT ME. IF WHATEVER'S OUT THERE CAN DO THIS, IF HE CAN ALTER TIME ITSELF...

...HOW CAN I FIGHT THAT?

"...YOU'LL TRACK IT DOWN."

JUSTICE LEAGUE WATCHTOWER.

"SOMETIMES YOU HAVE TO FOLLOW YOUR INSTINCTS. YOU KNOW THAT...

"...EVEN IF THEY SEEM EXTREME."

MY WIFE IS A *VERY SMART* WOMAN.

FLASH'S COSMIC TREADMILL.

HIS OWN PERSONAL TIME MACHINE.

HE ONCE SHOWED ME HOW TO SET THE TIME AND LOCATION.

IF FLASH CAN GO BACK IN TIME...

ACTION COMICS #986 variant cover by NEIL EDWARDS and JEROMY COX

ACTION COMICS #988 variant cover by NEIL EDWARDS and JEROMY COX

ACTION COMICS #989 variant cover by NEIL EDWARDS and JEROMY COX

Unused cover art for ACTION COMICS #987
with color by JASON WRIGHT

Unused cover art for ACTION COMICS #988
with color by BRAD ANDERSON

Issue Break-Downs:

- Part one:
    - Superman, hopeful of humanity and hearing positivity
    - Superman saving people from the usual man-made crises, oz agents teased in the mix.
    - Evident that the crises may be temporarily averted by Superman, but humanity will just slide right back
    - Man's capacity for evil highlighted
    - OZ's agents speak to Clark, call him to the fortress of solitude
    - OZ as Jor-El is revealed: "I'm sorry I sent you here"
- Part two:
    - Father and son meeting
    - Jor-El tells his tale, and the tale of the brutal ugliness of humanity
    - Jor El may have been blasted down to earth at one point, and experienced first hand how brutal humans can be
    - "you've been here too long, you're thinking like them"
    - Oz's agents are slowly moving into place to execute his grand plan
    - Oz to Superman: "you need to leave. Now."
- Part Three:
    - Oz visits Lois and Jon individually, makes his pitch.
    - Jon is tempted, grandpa's world is the promise of paradise and humanity is shown to be ugly and brutal
    - Superman rejects OZ's plan
    - Oz: "I didn't want to have to do this, but if you're not going to leave willingly I'll MAKE you leave"
- Part four:
    - Conflict over plan, Superman v. OZ
    - OZ unleashes his full power
    - "I'll show you how easy it is to corrupt humans" — his agents have been set up to bring about the end of the world
    - Superman succeeds in freeing OZ's agents and thwarting the plan, but humanity continues destroying itself on its own
    - Jon sides with OZ (or seems to)
- Part Five: similar pacing/beats to detective story
    - Superman v. OZ
    - Earth is saved, OZ is defeated
    - OZ is plucked away by a bright blue light, the experiment completed and sent to parts unknown.
    - Superman believes mr. oz to be dead, takes his staff and places it in the fortress
    - Superman is now doubtful in humanity, hearing negativity to echo pt1's opening – also echoes detective ending